KID SKILLS

Basketry

Build your skills with 20 great projects

Basketry

Build your skills with 20 great projects

DK

LONDON, NEW YORK,
MUNICH, MELBOURNE, DELHI

DTP Designer David McDonald
Special Sales Production Manager Silvia La Greca
Associate Publisher Nigel Duffield

The Book Makers
Author and Project Maker L. Foa
Project Manager Miranda Brown
Managing Editor Elise See Tai
Senior Designer Ali Scrivens
Photographer Andy Crawford
Consultant Eva Davies

We would also like to thank the following models for appearing in this book:
Corey O'Rourke, Bokai Sasay, Johannes Sasay-Wada, Callum Solomon, Jonah Winslett

First American Edition, 2009

Published in the United States by
DK Publishing, Inc.
375 Hudson Street,
New York, New York 10014

09 10 11 10 9 8 7 6 5 4 3 2 1

For more information on the Boy Scouts of America programs, visit www.scouting.org

A Cataloging-in-Publication record for this book is available from the Library of Congress.
ISBN 978-0-7566-5318-7

Color reproduction by MDP Ltd, UK
Printed and bound by Lake Book Manufacturing, USA

Discover more at
www.dk.com

Alerts, Tips, and Skills!

These appear throughout the book to offer extra help and advice. You can also keep track of how you're doing with the skill boxes.

! Alert

These warn of potential hazards when using particular tools or materials.

Craftsman's Tip

These give extra advice on tools, materials, and techniques.

Skill Learned

You will learn and practice new skills throughout this book. Check the box at the end of each project once you have mastered the skills!

CONTENTS

Baskets and Basketry

Welcome to basketry! Basket weaving is one of the world's most ancient crafts—from the beginning of civilization people have been gathering twigs, reeds, vines, and fibers and weaving them into useful containers of all shapes and sizes. Unlike many crafts that have altered with developing technologies, the art and techniques of basketry have changed little over time. With this book, you can build your basketry skills as you work through 20 awesome projects!

TYPES OF BASKET

Although baskets seem to come in a huge variety of designs, most start with one of relatively few basic structures. As you become familiar with the methods of weaving, you will begin to recognize the distinct way that each basket is made.

Wicker baskets

WICKER BASKETS
Wicker baskets are usually made with round reed but cane, willow, oak, and ash are also used.

Strips of reed make up the sides of this basket.

PLAITED BASKETS
These are created with flat, ribbon-like strips of reed passing over and under flat stakes.

RIBBED BASKETS
A sturdy skeleton is first created and then reed is woven around the skeleton to make the basket.

The skeleton has to be made first.

These baskets are coiled from the inside out.

COILED BASKETS
These baskets have no skeleton, or frame. A flexible core of pine needles or seagrass, for example, is wrapped with a soft material. This core is then coiled up, and the coils are sewn together to make a basket.

You can twine reed into a variety of shapes.

DIFFERENT SHAPES
Basketry techniques can also be used to make a range of objects other than baskets.

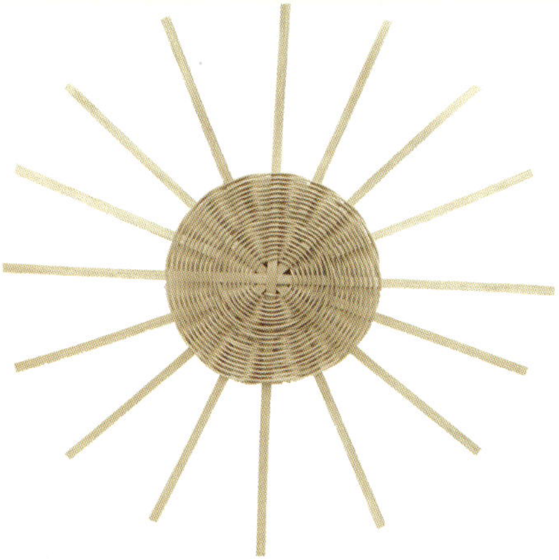

Reed is twined around and around.

TWINING
In this weaving, two weavers are used. One is taken over each stake, while the other is taken under it. The two weavers alternate in an over-under pattern all the way around the basket.

BASKETRY TECHNIQUES

The reed is woven in and out to make the basket.

OVER-UNDER, OR PLAIN, WEAVING
In this type of weaving, the weaver, which is the material that is woven around the basket, is taken over, then under the stakes, which are the part of the basket that the material is woven around.

TWILL WEAVING
This is similar to over-under weaving, but instead the weaver is taken over, then under, two or more stakes at a time.

START-STOP WEAVING
This weaving is done one row at a time and has to be done with an even number of stakes.

Start-stop weaving is perfect for making square shapes.

CONTINUOUS WEAVING
With this weaving, the weaver goes continuously around the basket and doesn't stop with each row. There must be an uneven number of stakes.

Weaving starts from the bottom and continues upward.

Basketry Materials

A huge range of natural materials, from grasses to vines to leaves to branches, can be woven into baskets. The most popular basketry material is reed, as it is readily available and easy to use. More traditional materials include willow, oak, and ash—these are valued for their beauty and durability, but are more difficult to work with than reed. Many other natural materials are woven into baskets, and some baskets are made with several different materials, creating interesting patterns and colorful styles.

REED

Reed is made from a vine-like plant called rattan, which is found in many rain forest areas. To turn rattan into reed, vines are pulled down from the forest canopy, chopped into long pieces, and sent to factories where they are cleaned and cut to size. Reed is available in two shapes—round and flat. It is generally sold in coils according to weight. You can buy coils of flat or round reed in craft stores and from furniture making and basket weaving supply stores.

Craftsman's Tip

If your reed dries out while you are weaving, you can dip it in a bucket of water, or spray it with water to dampen it. Don't leave it in water for too long as it will become slimy.

Coils of reed

3 mm round reed

2 mm round reed

1.5 mm round reed

Round reed is measured by diameter in millimeters, and is also classified by a number. For example, #1 round reed is 1.5 mm in diameter.

Flat reed is sold according to its width, which is measured in fractions of inches.

½" flat reed

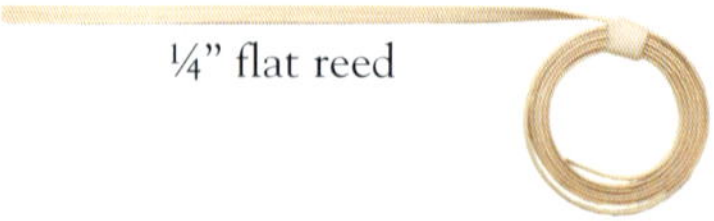
¼" flat reed

USING REED

When dry, reed is brittle and can snap easily. Always soak the reed before you weave to make it flexible and easy to use—soak it in water for three to five minutes. Thicker reed will need longer soaking than thinner reed. Take it out and pat it dry before you use it. Flat reed has a right (smooth) side and a wrong (splintery) side. Weave with the right side facing out.

WILLOW

Willow is a classic basket-making material. It is strong and long lasting and produces beautiful baskets. It is harder to work with than reed, and requires a much longer soaking time, but many basket makers believe that the end result is worth the extra effort.

BROWN WILLOW

This is willow that has been dried with its bark on. It is usually dark brown, and is springy to work with.

GREEN WILLOW

This is freshly cut willow. It is soft and flexible, and doesn't need to be soaked. However, it dries out in a few weeks (and turns into brown willow), and is therefore only available during the willow harvest period.

BUFF WILLOW

This willow is boiled in its bark for several hours, which turns the rods a rusty brown color, called buff, and makes the bark easy to remove. The bark is then peeled off, leaving a strong, flexible rod. Buff willow is the most commonly used willow for basketry as it is relatively easy to use.

Willow wall

WHITE WILLOW

These rods have the bark removed without boiling them first, leaving them a creamy white color. This is only possible for a short period in spring, so it is not always available.

USING WILLOW

Willow is usually sold in bolts. A bolt is a bundle of rods of the same length, which has a circumference of about 3 ft. 2 in, at its base. Willow is brittle when it is dry and will break when it is bent, so it must be soaked before it is used. Buff and white willow should be soaked in cold water for one to three hours, and then wrapped in a damp cloth and left for several hours so that the cores of the willow rods also become flexible. Brown willow needs to be soaked for several days.

OTHER MATERIALS

A huge range of other materials are woven into baskets, creating baskets with every imaginable style, color, pattern, and texture.

Pine needles can be used as a flexible core in coiled baskets.

Pine needles

Raffia is a soft, paper-like material, which is torn into thin strips. It is very strong and is often dyed in bright colors.

This woven raffia has been dyed.

Seagrass

Seagrass is a strong material, which is often used in basketry projects.

Your Tools and How to Use Them

Traditionally, basket makers need very few tools to make baskets—the essential tools are those used to prepare the materials, such as water containers to soak the reed and scissors to cut it to size. Other tools, such as binder clips and awls are not essential, but sometimes make the weaving process easier and the end result neater.

Binder clips: Binder clips are useful when you want to clip stakes to your work surface (to hold them in position), or to hold pieces of reed together as you weave.

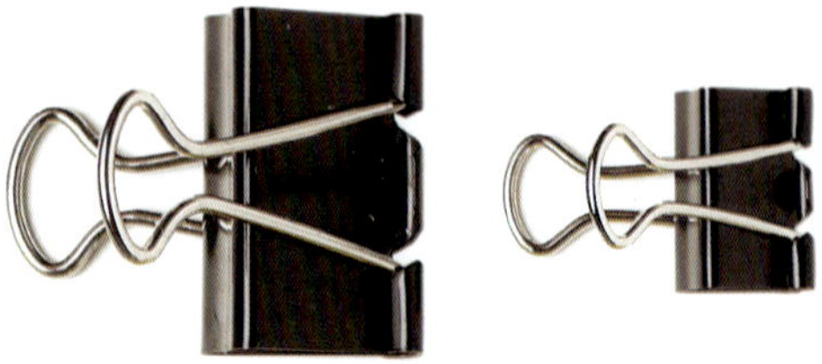

Binder clips

MEASURING AND MARKING

Pencil and ruler: These are useful when preparing basketry materials, as they are used to measure and mark the materials. A tape measure is also useful for measuring larger pieces of material.

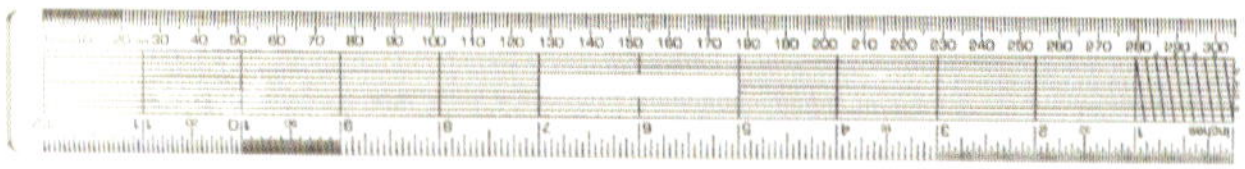

A 12" ruler can be used to measure your stakes.

Pencil

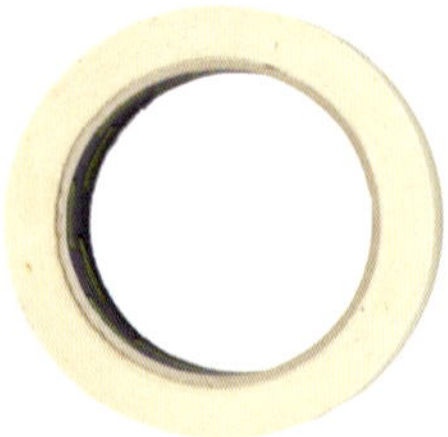

Masking tape

Masking tape: Tape is often useful to hold the stakes in place, while weaving a basket base.

SOAKING YOUR MATERIALS

It is essential that reed and willow are soaked before they are used. Reed can be placed in a bucket or large bowl for a few minutes, while willow needs to be soaked in a large container, such as a bathtub, for hours or even days. A spray bottle can be used to keep the materials damp while you work.

Large bowl, spray bottle, and towel

CUTTING AND TRIMMING

Scissors: Sharp scissors can be used to cut both round and flat reed, and to trim stray bits of reed on your finished projects.

Sharp scissors

Pruning shears

Pruning shears: These are mainly used to cut branches and twigs and are important when working with tougher materials, such as willow.

EXTRA TOOLS

Awl: An awl is often used to create space within the weave to insert extra stakes, or tuck in the weavers. If you don't have an awl available, you can use a screwdriver for the same purpose.

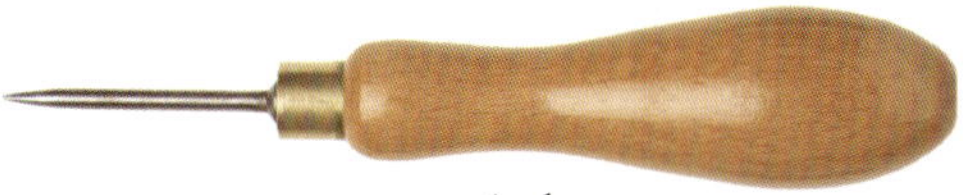

Awl

Pliers: Pliers are not essential, but are sometimes useful for pulling weavers through when weaving. They are also useful when bending willow stakes into an upright position.

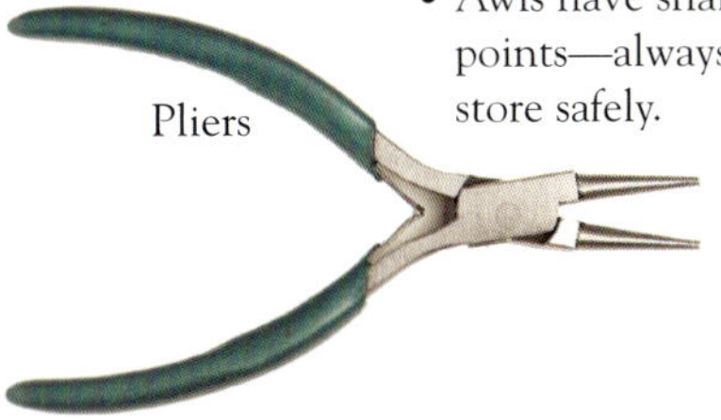

Pliers

Seagrass needle

Seagrass needle: This needle is used when working with seagrass—it makes weaving with seagrass much easier.

Paints

Paintbrush and paints: There are a variety of paint colors available that can be used to add color to the reed. The reed is usually painted before it is woven.

! Alert

- Always point scissors away from you when using them.
- Pruning shears are very sharp—use caution with shears.
- Awls have sharp points—always store safely.

GLUING AND STICKING

Glue: This isn't an essential material for basketry, but glue is useful for certain projects, where the materials need to be secured together before the weaving starts. For example, to make a ribbed basket, you need to start with a skeleton, where the skeleton shape is first glued together before the material is twined around it.

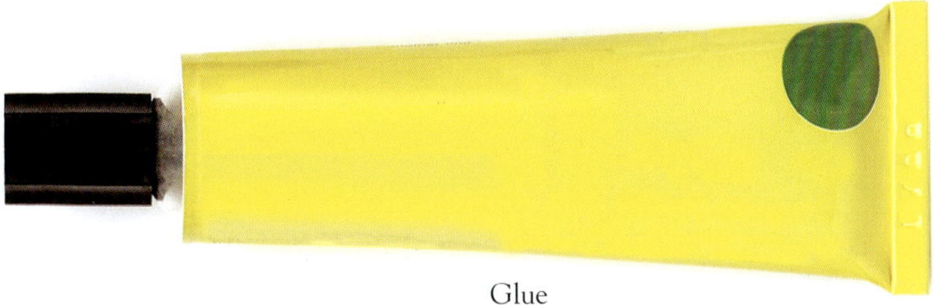

Glue

Handy Bulletin Board

THIS STYLISH BULLETIN board is the perfect place to keep all your notes and photos! This is a simple introduction to working with reed and using the over-under weaving technique. We'll be gluing strips of flat reed onto cardboard in a simple crisscross pattern to create a board for your wall. Tuck important papers into the weave to keep them safe. Once you have learned the technique, you can experiment with your own designs and different sizes.

WHAT YOU NEED

TOOLS AND MATERIALS

- Pencil
- Ruler
- Sharp scissors
- Binder clips
- Colored cardboard, measuring 20" x 16"
- *Soak reed before using it*
- ¼" flat reed
- Glue

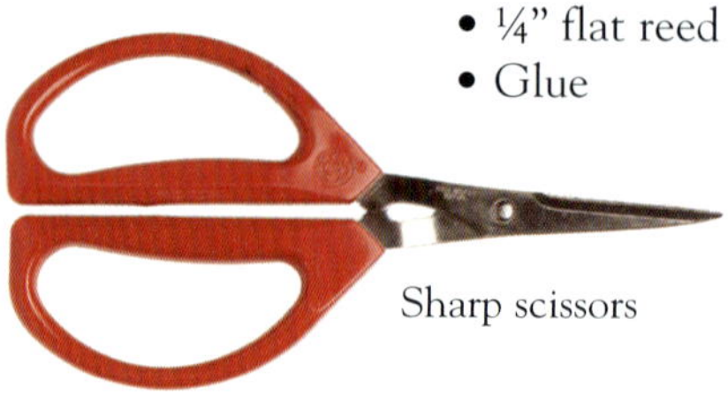

Sharp scissors

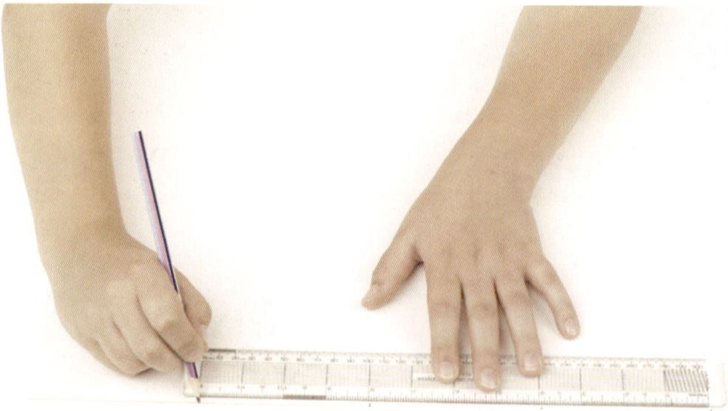

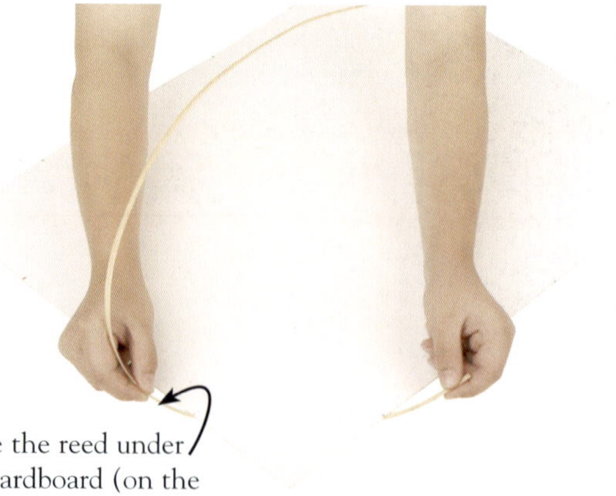

Place the reed under the cardboard (on the colored side).

1 Make a mark every 4" along each edge of the back of the cardboard. Place strips of reed in water for a few minutes. Then, pat them dry with a towel.

2 At 1 corner of the cardboard, place a strip of reed underneath, so that the ends poke out at the first 2 marks. Trim the reed so that about 1" of reed pokes out at each end.

Glue the ends of the reed down on the back of the cardboard.

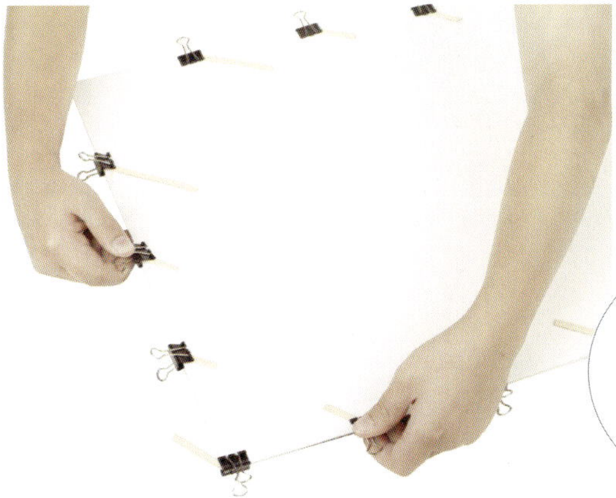

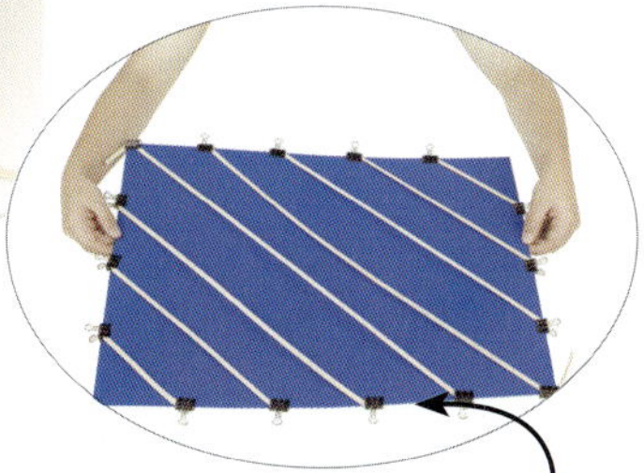

The reed strips should look like this on the front of the cardboard.

3 Fold the reed over at the marks and glue it down. Use binder clips to hold the reed in place, while the glue dries.

4 Continue adding strips all the way along the cardboard in the same way. Check that each strip is parallel to the last strip before you glue the reed down.

! Alert

- Always point scissors away from you when using them.

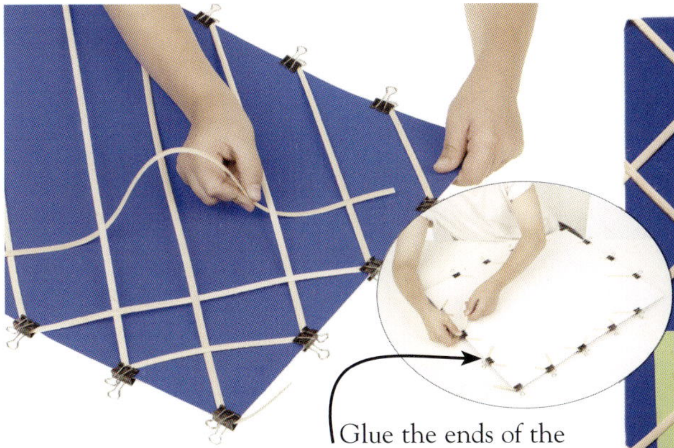

Glue the ends of the strips down on the back of the cardboard.

5 Now glue strips in the opposite direction. Weave the strips under and over the strips already glued down as shown. Glue the ends of the strips down in the same way as before.

When all the strips are glued down, your bulletin board is complete! Hang it in your room and tuck important notes and photos under the reed.

Skill Learned

- Soaking reed
- Simple over-under weaving
- Gluing reed

Cool Checkerboard

WE'LL BE BUILDING our over-under weaving skills to create a cool checkerboard in this project. The checkerboard is made using a simple over-under pattern—we'll learn how to weave the shape for the board, and paint on bright-colored squares. Use small coins as pieces and then you're ready to play—challenge your friends to a cool checker championship!

WHAT YOU NEED

TOOLS AND MATERIALS

- Pencil
- Ruler
- Sharp scissors
- Binder clips
- Paintbrush
- *Soak reed before using it*
- 24, 10" strips of ½" flat reed
- 4, 12" strips of ½" flat reed
- Glue
- Paints

Weave the second strip over the first reed, then under the next 2, and over the next 2, to the end.

Craftsman's Tip

Start your project by cutting the flat reed into the correct number of strips, to the correct length.

1 Glue 16 of the 10" strips along the top of a 12" strip as shown. Hold the pieces in place with binder clips, while the glue dries.

2 Weave a 10" strip parallel to the 12" strip, going under the first reed, over the next 2, under the next 2, and so on to the end. Then, weave the next strip as shown.

3 Repeat step 2 with 6 more strips of 10" reed. You can keep a gap in between these rows.

4 Turn the board over and glue the 12" strips along the bottom and sides of the board. Clip them in place and wait for the glue to dry.

! Alert

- Always point scissors away from you when using them.

Skill Learned

- Creating a flat woven square
- Painting reed

5 Trim the ends and paint squares onto the board as shown. Paint 16 small coins 1 color and 16 small coins another color to use as pieces on your board.

Sunshine Sun Decoration

LEARN A NEW weaving technique and create a sparkling sun! Hang it in your window for sunshine all day long. This project teaches you how to make a "star" base, which is a circular basket base, and introduces a weaving technique called twining. Once you have mastered the technique, you'll be able to create a range of baskets. We'll also be using some basketry terms—"weaver," the material you weave with, and "spoke," the part of the basket that you weave around.

WHAT YOU NEED

TOOLS AND MATERIALS

- Pencil
- Ruler
- Sharp scissors
- Binder clips
- Paintbrush
- *Soak reed before using it*
- 8, 20" pieces of ½" flat reed (spokes)
- 2.75 mm round reed (weaver)
- Gold paint

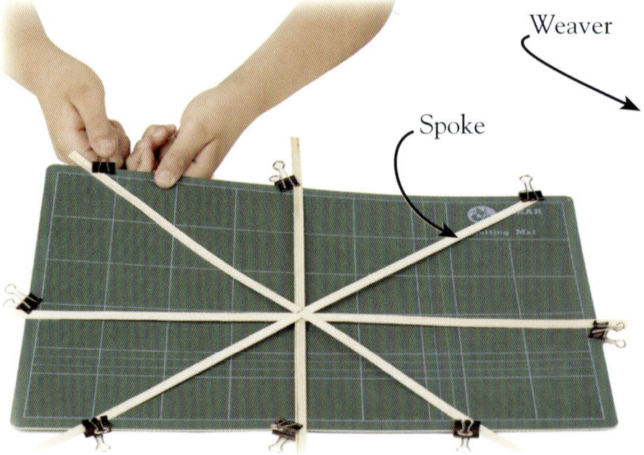

Craftsman's Tip

Spokes and stakes are the same thing, but spokes are usually laid out like spokes of a wheel.

1 Mark the middle of all the spokes and lay 4 of them in a star shape as shown. Clip or tape them onto the work surface, with the center marks aligned. Soak the weaver.

2 Fold the weaver in half and place half of it under 1 of the spokes as shown. Take the bottom piece of weaver over the next spoke and the top piece under the spoke.

In twining, you take the lower weaver over the next spoke, and the upper weaver under the next spoke.

3 This under-over weaving is called "twining." Twine all the way around the star shape and keep going around and around until you have twined 8 rows.

4 Place 4 new spokes in the gaps between the stakes. Continue twining and twine 10 rows around all of the spokes.

5 Tuck the ends of the weaver into the weave and trim any reed that is sticking out and the ends of the spokes. Paint your sun gold to finish.

Stick your sun on a wall, or hang it in a window.

! Alert

- Always point scissors away from you when using them.

Craftsman's Tip

If you run out of weaver, place a new piece next to the old weaver, a few spokes before it will run out. Twine with both weavers until the old weaver runs out and continue twining with the new weaver. Try to keep all of the ends on the side of the weave facing you.

Skill Learned

- Making a circular "star" base
- Twining

Round Wastepaper Basket

THIS BRIGHT BASKET is both fun to make and practical to use—use it to add a splash of color to your room, and to keep your room clean and tidy! This project builds on the sun's circular base, and introduces you to continuous weaving and lashing a rim together. Once you've got the hang of it, you can make more baskets for different purposes—have a try at the plant pot holder on the next page!

WHAT YOU NEED

TOOLS AND MATERIALS

- Pencil
- Ruler
- Sharp scissors
- Binder clips
- Awl
- Paintbrush

- *Soak reed before using it*
- 8, 30" pieces of ½" flat reed (spokes)
- 3 mm round reed (weaver for the base)
- ½" flat reed (weaver for the sides)
- 3/8" flat reed (lasher for rim)
- Seagrass
- Paints

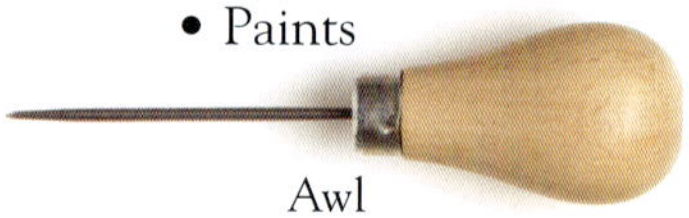

Awl

Craftsman's Tip

To protect your work surface, place scrap paper or newspaper under your reed when painting.

1 Paint the long strips of flat reed for the sides in bright colors. Leave the reed to dry. Follow steps 1–5 of the sun decoration instructions for weaving the base of your basket.

2 Cut 1 of the spokes in half down its middle. Then, dampen the spokes and fold them back on themselves as shown.

! Alert

- Always point scissors away from you when using them.

3 Clip 1 of your colored weavers onto the outside of 1 of the spokes and weave around the shape, going under and over each spoke in turn, so that you complete 1 row.

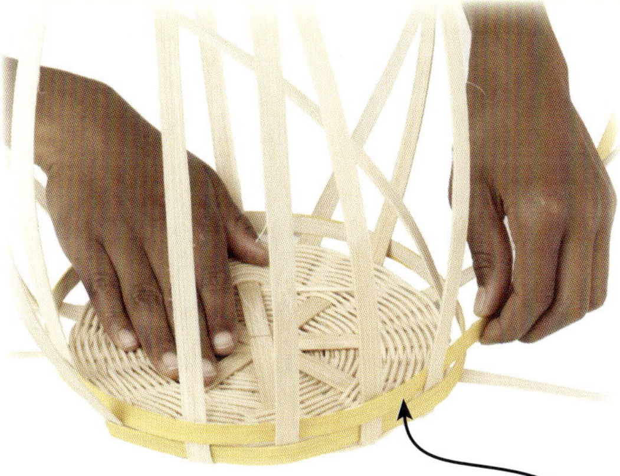

When you have completed the first row, continue weaving.

4 Continue weaving on to the second row. The weaver should go over the spokes it went under in the last row, and under the spokes it went over. This is "continuous weaving."

Start with the end of the new weaver on the inside of 1 of the spokes.

5 When you have nearly run out of weaver, overlap it with another colored weaver for 2 spokes and continue weaving with this new weaver.

Cut off the tops of the spokes that are on the inside.

6 Weave 25 rows with different colors. Trim the tops of the spokes that are on the inside of the top row of the weave. Then, dampen the tops of the remaining spokes.

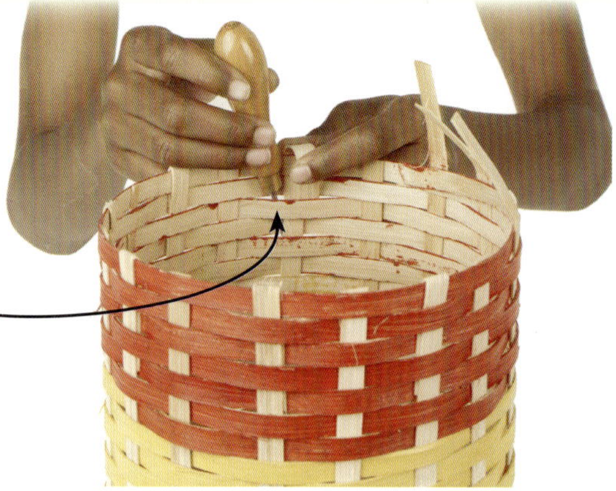

Use an awl to make space for the spokes to be tucked in.

Craftsman's Tip

If you don't have an awl, you can use a screwdriver to make space between the weave.

7 Fold the remaining spokes down and tuck them into the weave as shown. Cut off any ends.

8 To add the rim, clip a piece of colored weaver around the top of the outside of the basket and another along the inside as shown. Then, place a piece of seagrass along the top.

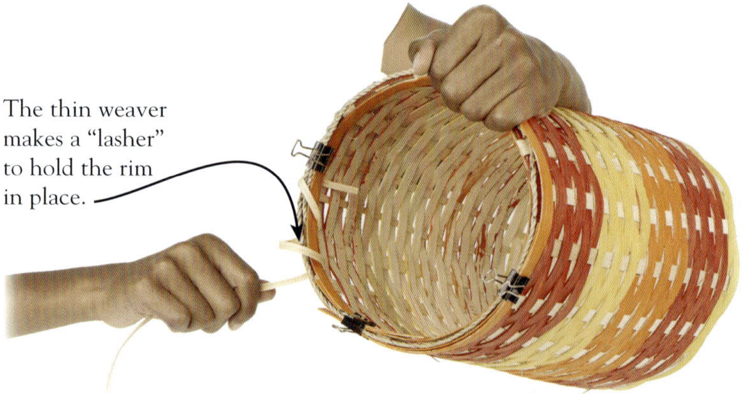

The thin weaver makes a "lasher" to hold the rim in place.

9 Lash the rim together using a thin weaver (lasher)—tuck the end into the rim, and loop the other end around the rim and through the top row of the weave.

10 Go around the whole rim in the same way, wrapping the weaver around the rim and the top row. Tuck the lasher in at the end.

! Alert

- Awls have sharp points—always store safely.

Perfect Plant Pot

Put your basket-making skills to the test and make a plant pot for your next project.

Skill Learned

- Making a simple basket
- Continuous weaving
- Lashing a rim together

Terrific Toy Basket

MAKE A HUGE basket to store all your toys and games! This project uses the same method as the wastepaper basket, but here, the base is much larger and the sides slope outward, creating a completely different effect. Decorate your basket by adding colorful beads as you weave. Once you have learned the technique, you can make baskets to solve all your storage needs!

WHAT YOU NEED

TOOLS AND MATERIALS

- Pencil
- Ruler
- Sharp scissors
- Awl

- *Soak reed before using it*
- 8, 50" pieces of ½" flat reed (spokes for base)
- 15, 20" pieces of ½" flat reed (spokes for base)
- 3.5 mm round reed (weaver for base and sides)
- 186 beads (with holes that 3.5 mm round reed can fit through)
- ½" flat reed (weaver for sides)
- Seagrass
- 1.5 mm round reed (lasher for rim)

Store all your stuff in your basket.

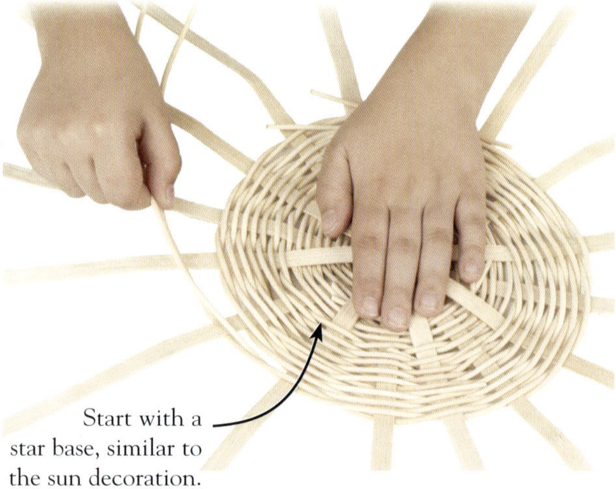

Start with a star base, similar to the sun decoration.

1 Begin with a star base—arrange 4 long spokes in a star shape and twine around them for 7 rows. Place 4 more long spokes in the gaps and twine around all the spokes for 9 more rows.

2
Tuck the 15 shorter spokes into all the gaps between the old spokes except 1. Twine around the whole base for 5 more rows.

3
Dampen and fold all of the spokes back on themselves. Weave around the sides of the basket with flat reed by continuous weaving for 6 rows.

See the wastepaper basket project for adding a rim.

4
Fold the round reed in half and place it over the next spoke along. Twine all the way around, adding 3 beads to 1 side of the weaver every time you twine passed a stake.

5
Twine around once more without beads. Follow with 10 rows of flat reed, then 2 rows of twining with the round weaver and beads, and finally 3 rows of flat reed. Add a rim to finish.

! Alert
- Always point scissors away from you when using them.
- Awls have sharp points—always store safely.

Skill Learned
- Twining using beads
- Twining and continuous weaving

Pen and Pencil Holder

MAKE A TALL container that's perfect for all your pencils and pens! This project begins with a different type of circular base—the "stakes," the part of the basket that you weave around, are first woven together in a cross shape, and then gradually separated by weaving into a circular shape. Learn how to twine the sides of this basket to create a neat, woven effect.

WHAT YOU NEED

TOOLS AND MATERIALS

- Pencil
- Ruler
- Sharp scissors
- Rubber band
- Awl
- Binder clips

- *Soak reed before using it*
- 8, 20" pieces of 3 mm round reed (stakes for base)
- 3 mm round reed (weaver for base and sides)
- ½" flat reed (rim)
- 1.5 mm round reed (lasher for rim)
- Masking tape

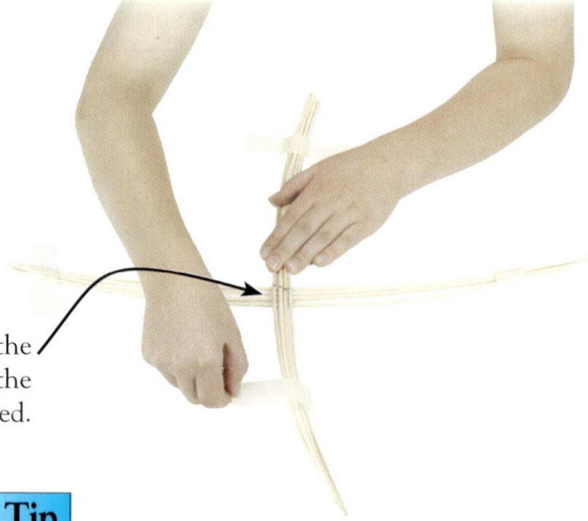

Make sure the centers of the stakes are aligned.

Craftsman's Tip

Remember that a weaver is often folded in half, creating a top and a bottom half—sometimes referred to as 2 weavers.

1 Mark the centers of the stakes and dampen them in water for a few minutes. Place 4 stakes horizontally, and 4 stakes vertically on top of them. Tape the stakes to the work surface.

2 Fold the weaver in half. Place the weaver over the top 4 stakes, with 1 half under and 1 half over the stakes. Pull the fold to the edge of the stakes.

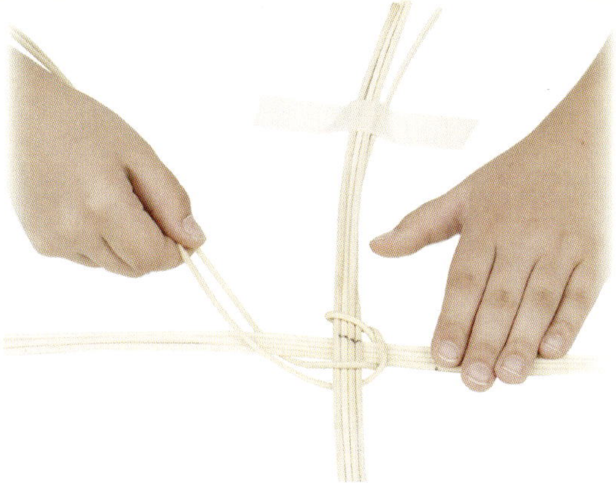

3 Take the top part of the weaver under the next 4 stakes and the bottom part over the next 4 stakes. Twine around the stakes, swapping the sides of the weaver every 4 stakes.

4 Twine around the shape for 4 rows. Then, create 2 more rows, swapping the sides of the weaver every 2 stakes.

! Alert

- Always point scissors away from you when using them.

5 Create 2 more rows, but this time swap the sides of the weaver every stake. Tuck the ends of the weaver into the base.

6 If you run out of weaver at any point, take a new piece and overlap it with the old weaver for 2 stakes, and continue twining with the new weaver.

Craftsman's Tip

A rubber band keeps the stakes together so that you can twine around them more easily. You can remove the rubber band once you have twined a few rows and the pen holder begins to take shape.

7 Dampen the stakes. Then, fold them back on themselves as shown.

8 Hold the stakes upright with a rubber band. Fold the weaver in half and twine it around the stakes.

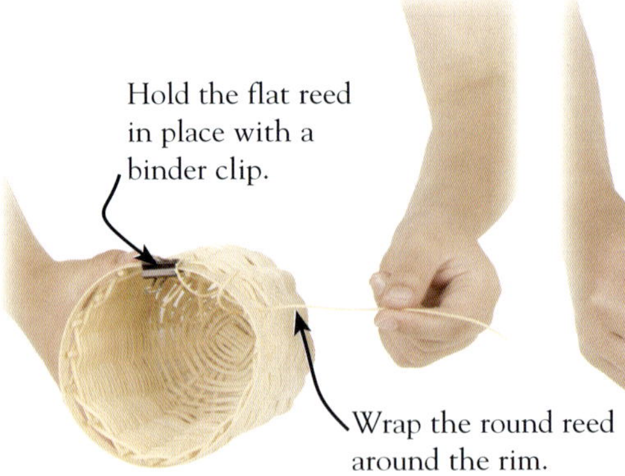

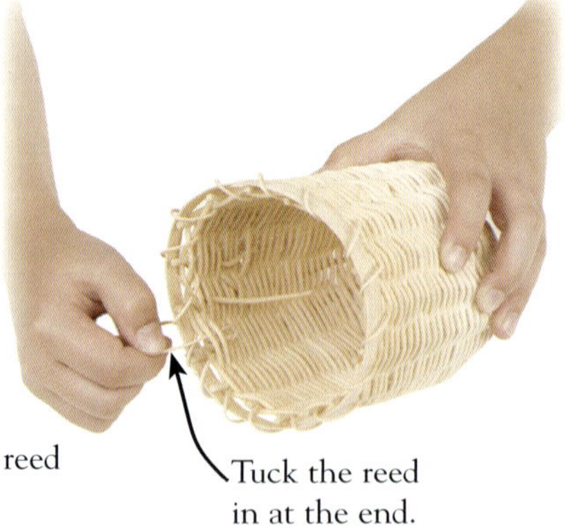

Craftsman's Tip

Don't forget to trim the tops of the stakes before you secure the rim with the round reed.

9 Twine for 25 rows. Then, tuck the weaver in at the top.

10 Wrap a piece of flat reed around the top for the rim and cut it so that it overlaps itself at the end. Then, loop the round reed lasher around the rim to secure it.

Store all your pens and pencils in your perfect round pen and pencil holder!

! Alert

- Awls have sharp points—always store safely.

Skill Learned

- Making a circular "cross" base
- Twining the sides of a basket

Water Bottle Holder

CREATE A COOL striped design by weaving with both reed and seagrass in this project. Make a basket to hold your water bottle and add a seagrass strap so that you can carry it with you wherever you go! The combination of seagrass and reed creates a great effect that you can experiment with for your own projects.

WHAT YOU NEED

TOOLS AND MATERIALS

- Pencil
- Ruler
- Sharp scissors
- Rubber band
- Awl
- *Soak reed before using it*
- 8, 25" pieces of 3 mm round reed (stakes)
- 3 mm round reed (weaver)
- Seagrass
- Masking tape

1 Make the base of the water bottle holder in the same way as the pen holder. Twine the rows until the base is just a little bigger than the bottom of your bottle.

Tuck all the stakes in, in the same direction.

4 Dampen the stakes and tuck each stake into the space next to the next stake along as shown.

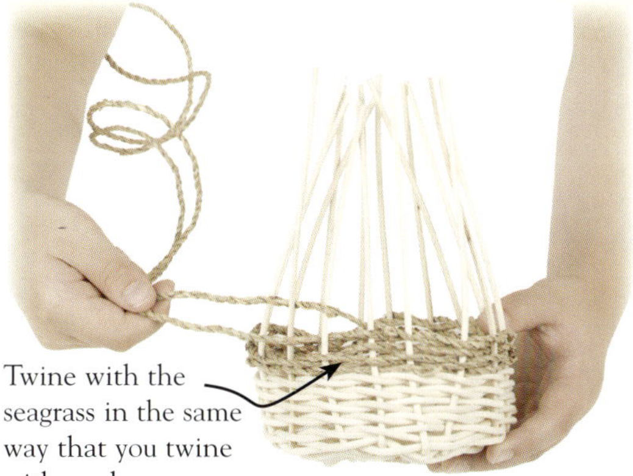

Twine with the seagrass in the same way that you twine with reed.

2 Fold the stakes up and twine 5 rows using round reed. Tuck the ends in, and then twine 4 rows with seagrass.

3 Twine 4 rows of reed, then 4 rows of seagrass until the bottle holder is as tall as your water bottle.

You may need to use an awl to help you to tuck in your seagrass handle.

5 Attach a strap by doubling over a length of seagrass, pushing each end through the top rows of weaving and tying a knot to hold the ends in place.

! Alert

- Always point scissors away from you when using them.
- Awls have sharp points—always store safely.

Craftsman's Tip

Twining with seagrass is the same as twining with reed—fold the seagrass in half and place it over 1 of the stakes. Then, take the outer piece inside the next stake and the inner piece outside of the next stake and continue.

Skill Learned

- Twining with seagrass
- Adding a handle

Ball Game Bat

WEAVE A PADDLE-SHAPED bat for the first part of this cool ball game! The second part of this game is a set of color-coded baskets, which will follow this project. We'll be using some of our twining skills to make a different shape for the bat here. Once you have learned the technique, you can experiment and practice your skills to create your own shapes using your new basketry skills.

WHAT YOU NEED

TOOLS AND MATERIALS

- Pencil
- Ruler
- Sharp scissors
- *Soak reed before using it*
- 4, 12" pieces of 4 mm round reed (stakes)
- 4, 20" pieces of 4 mm round reed (stakes)
- 2 mm round reed (weaver)
- Masking tape

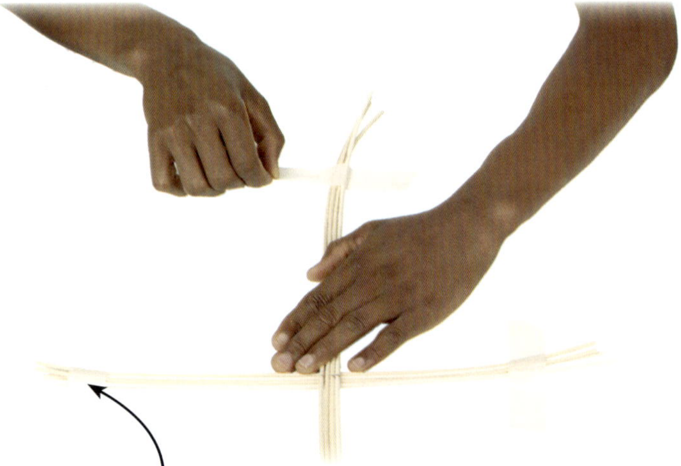

Tape the stakes to your work surface.

1 Mark the centers of the short stakes and mark 6" from the top of the long stakes. Position the short stakes horizontally and the long stakes vertically, with all marks aligned.

2 Twine around the stakes in the same way as the pen pot. Twine around 4 stakes at a time for 2 rows. Separate the top and side stakes into groups of 2—twine around them twice.

! Alert

- Always point scissors away from you when using them.

3 Separate the top and side stakes and twine around them 1 stake at a time, keeping the bottom 4 stakes together. Twine 15 rows.

4 For the bat handle, separate the bottom 4 stakes into groups of 2 and twine around them, folding the weavers back on themselves at the sides of the handle.

5 Weave 20 rows in this way, then separate the stakes into singles and weave around them for 8 rows. Tuck the weaver into the weave.

Craftsman's Tip

Use a bucket of water to dampen your bat before tucking the ends of the stakes in.

Skill Learned

- Making a bat
- Following a pattern to make a different shape

6 Dampen the bat. Tuck the ends of the stakes into the weave as shown—tuck each stake in, next to the next stake along.

7 Tie the bottom stakes together as shown and trim off any ends.

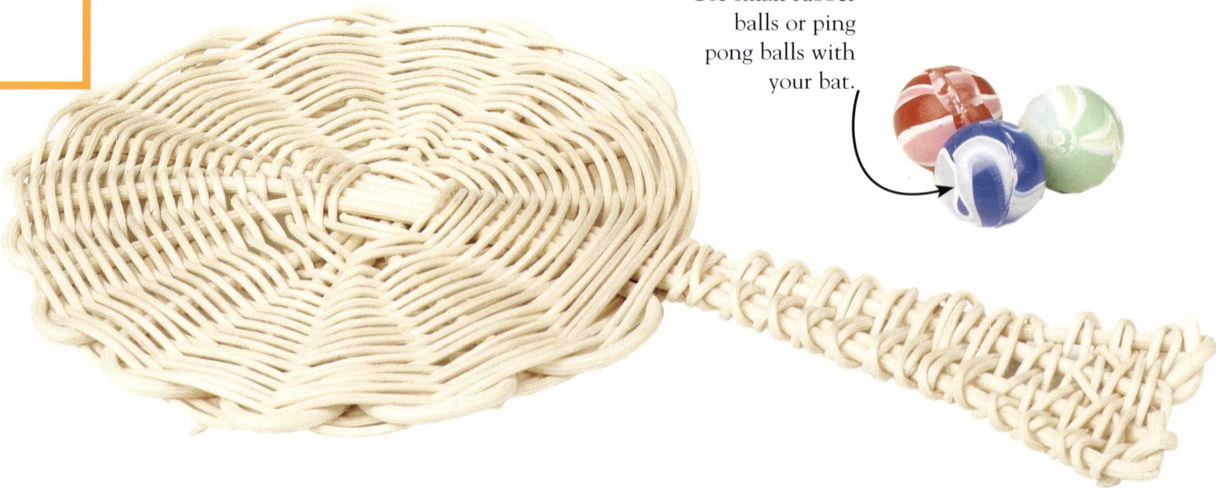

Use small rubber balls or ping pong balls with your bat.

Ball Game Baskets

WE'LL BE MAKING the baskets for our ball game here. Once you've made your bat and baskets, place the baskets on the floor, or hang them on a wall, and see if you can hit balls into them using your bat. You will score 10 points for hitting the ball into the smallest basket, 7 points for the middle basket, and 5 points for the largest basket—it's not as easy as it looks!

WHAT YOU NEED

TOOLS AND MATERIALS

- Pencil
- Ruler
- Sharp scissors
- Paintbrush

- *Soak reed before using it*
- 4, 20" pieces of ½" flat reed (spokes for 1 basket)
- 2 mm round reed (weaver for base)
- ¼" flat reed (weaver for sides)
- ½" flat reed (colored weaver for sides)
- 3/8" flat reed (lasher for rim)
- Seagrass
- Paints

! Alert

- Always point scissors away from you when using them.

1 Paint a long strip of ½" flat reed and leave it to dry.

2 Create a star base following steps 1–3 of the sun decoration—lie the spokes down in a star shape and twine around them for 8 rows.

3 Dampen the spokes and fold them back on themselves. Cut 1 of the spokes down its middle.

4 Weave around the spokes using continuous weaving (see steps 3 and 4 of the wastepaper basket). Weave 10 rows.

Craftsman's Tip

See the wastepaper basket project for weaving the baskets for your ball game.

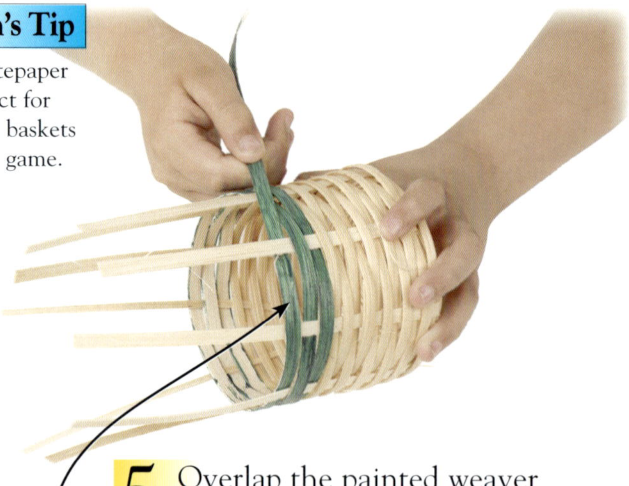

Weave 3 rows with your painted weaver.

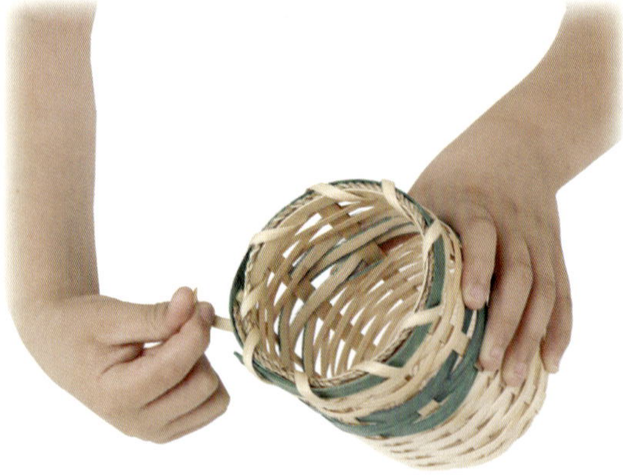

5 Overlap the painted weaver with the unpainted weaver for 2 spokes. Cut off the unpainted weaver and continue weaving with the painted weaver from this point. Weave 3 rows.

6 Switch back to the plain weaver and weave 5 more rows. Follow steps 6–10 of the wastepaper basket to cut off and fold the stakes at the top, and to add a colored rim.

Make 2 more baskets in different sizes by altering the number of rows you twine for the bases.

Craftsman's Tip

We have created a small basket with 5 rows twined for the base and a larger basket with 14 rows twined for the base.

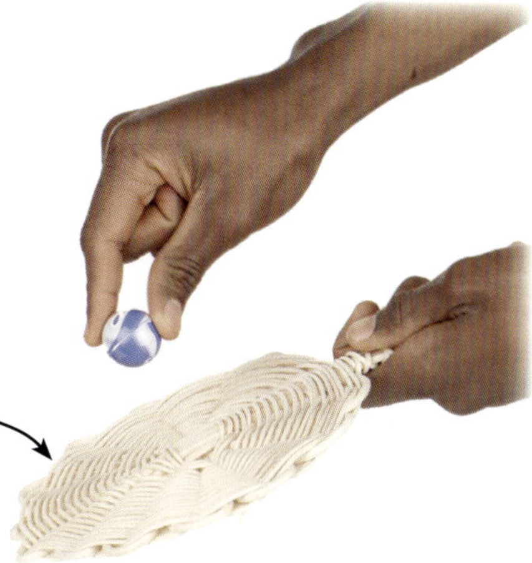

See if you can hit the ball into the basket.

How to play the game:

Hang the baskets from hooks on a wall or sit them on the floor and use your bat to try to hit balls into the baskets. Balls that go into the smallest basket score 10 points, the middle basket scores 7 points, and the largest basket scores 5 points.

Skill Learned

- Making different sized baskets

Handy Binoculars Pouch

CREATE A POUCH that fits your binoculars perfectly, so that you can carry them when you go on a hike! In this project, we'll see how to make an oval-shaped basket, using similar principles to those used for the pen holder. Once you have seen how changing the base alters the shape of a basket, see what wacky designs you can create!

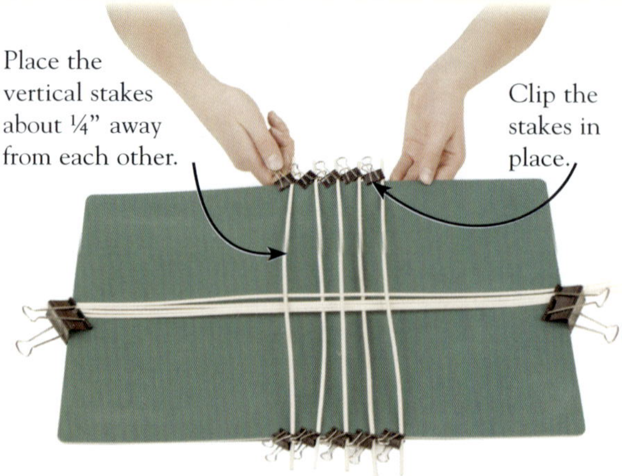

1 Mark the centers of the stakes. Place 4 long stakes horizontally and a 14" stake across the center. Place a stake on either side, under the horizontal stakes and 2 more stakes above them.

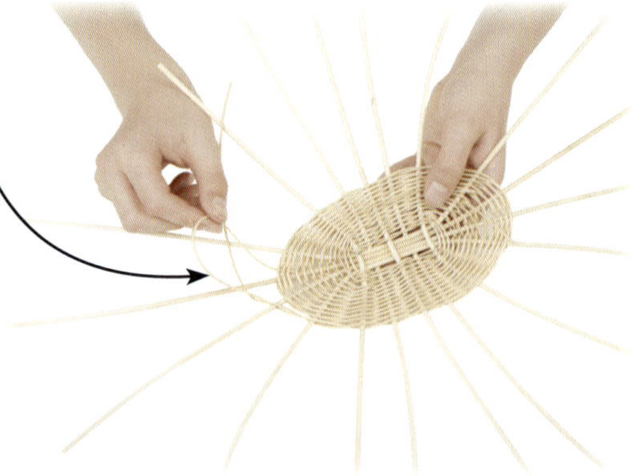

4 Twine around all the stakes individually. Twine 18 rows, or until the base is wide enough for your binoculars. Tuck in the ends of the weaver.

WHAT YOU NEED

TOOLS AND MATERIALS

- Ruler
- Pencil
- Sharp scissors
- Binder clips
- Awl

- *Soak reed before using it*
- 4, 20" pieces of 3 mm round reed (horizontal stakes)
- 5, 14" pieces of 3 mm round reed (vertical stakes)
- 1.5 mm round reed (weaver for base)
- 3 mm round reed (weaver for sides)
- Seagrass (for handle)

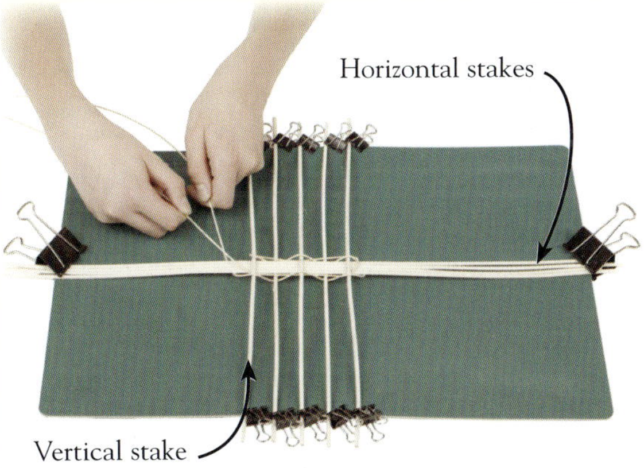

2 Fold the 1.5 mm weaver in half and start twining around base. Twine around the vertical stakes individually, and the horizontal stakes 4 at a time.

3 Twine 3 rows and then separate out the horizontal stakes.

! Alert

- Always point scissors away from you when using them.

Craftsman's Tip

You can unclip your stakes once they are held in position by the weave.

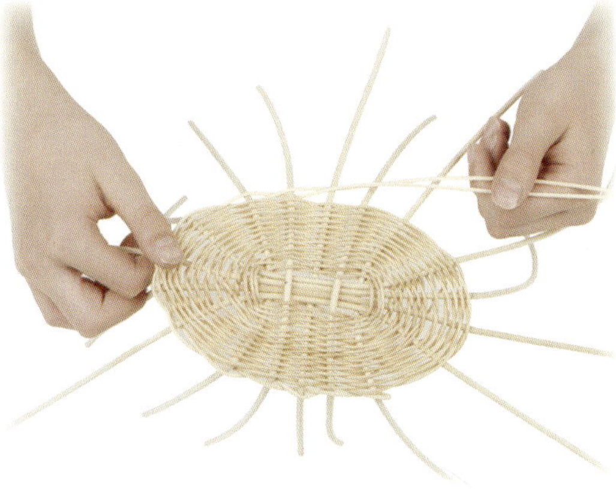

5 Dampen the stakes and bend them back on themselves. Start twining the sides using the 3 mm round weaver in the same way as you did for the pen holder.

6 Twine 16 rows or to the height of your binoculars. Tuck in the ends of the weaver.

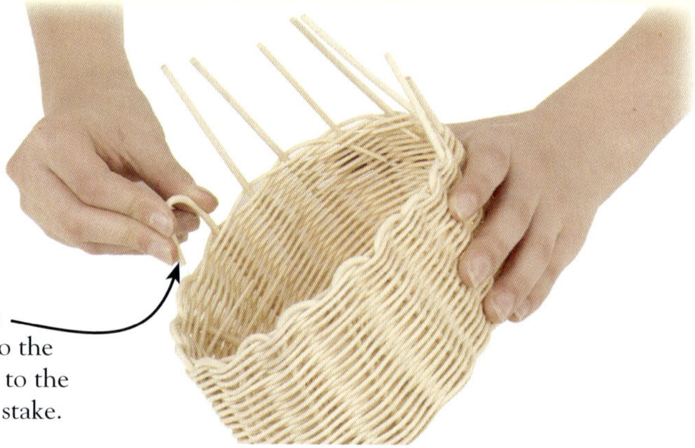

7 Tuck in the ends of the stakes as shown. Trim off any ends.

8 Push 3 strands of seagrass through 1 side of the basket and knot the ends together.

9 Braid the strands of seagrass and then push them through the other side of the basket. Knot the ends of the strands together.

10 Knot a piece of seagrass on either side of the middle of the basket. These can be tied together to hold your binoculars in the pouch.

Place your binoculars in the holder, tie the seagrass together to hold them in place, put the seagrass handle over your shoulder, and you're ready to go!

! Alert

- Awls have sharp points—always store safely.

Skill Learned

- Making an oval base
- Shaping the base to fit an object

Tidy CD Box

THIS SQUARE BOX is ideal for keeping your CDs in order! Make a square base, and learn a new weaving technique called start-stop weaving in this project. Square boxes are a simple, elegant way to store your stuff—make a few boxes in different sizes and use them as storage solutions! You can also get your paints out and paint the reed to create a range of colorful boxes. You can even try making a rectangular box!

WHAT YOU NEED
TOOLS AND MATERIALS

- Pencil
- Ruler
- Sharp scissors
- Binder clips
- Awl
- *Soak reed before using it*
- 18, 20" pieces of ½" flat reed (stakes)
- ¼" flat reed (weaver)
- Masking tape

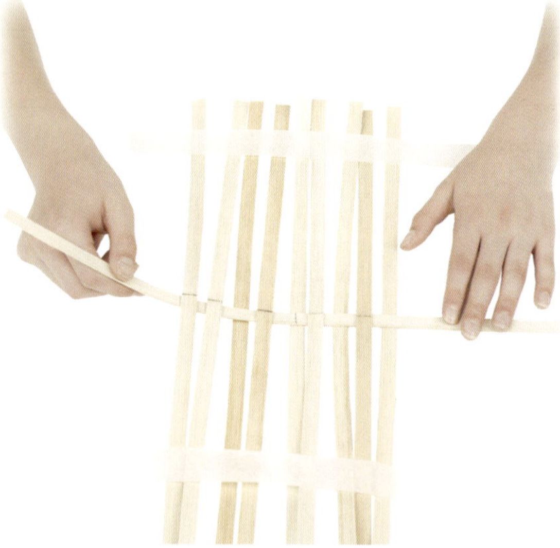

1 Mark the centers of all the stakes. Lay 9 stakes horizontally, about ¼" apart with the centers aligned. Tape or clip them in place.

2 Thread a stake along the center marks, weaving over and under the horizontal stakes.

3 Thread 4 stakes on either side of the center stake. When adding a new stake, take it under the stakes the previous stake went over, and over the stakes the previous stake went under.

4 Wet the stakes. Then, fold them back on themselves as shown.

! Alert

- Always point scissors away from you when using them.

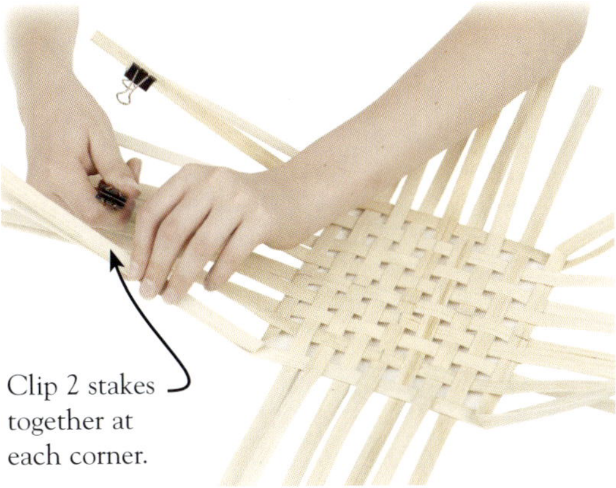

Clip 2 stakes together at each corner.

5 Use binder clips to clip the corner stakes together.

Starting with 2 lengths of weaver, makes it easier to start the sides of the box.

6 Start weaving the sides. Begin with 2 lengths of weaver. Clip 1 in front of a center stake and the other just above it behind that stake.

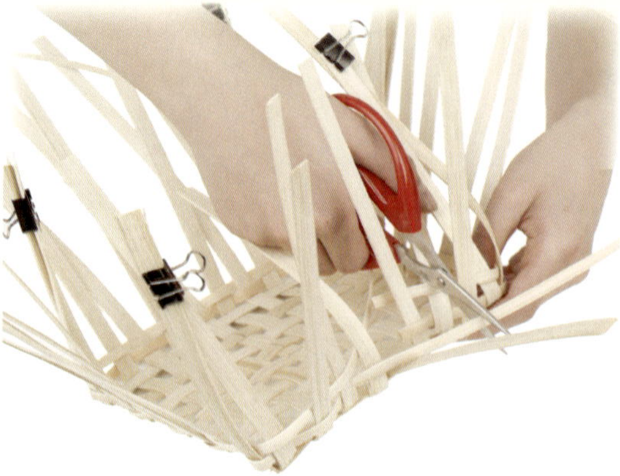

Craftsman's Tip

Start each new row on the next side along. This stops 1 side of the basket becoming too bulky.

7 Weave each weaver around the base in an over-under fashion.

8 When you have woven back to the start, continue weaving with the bottom weaver for a few stakes so that the reed overlaps. Cut the weaver and tuck the end inside the basket.

Use a new weaver for each new row.

9 Repeat for the second weaver. Then, add a new weaver. Start from the next side along, weave around the sides, and then overlap it for a couple of stakes before cutting it.

10 Add 15 rows of weaving to the base in the same way. This type of weaving is called "start-stop weaving."

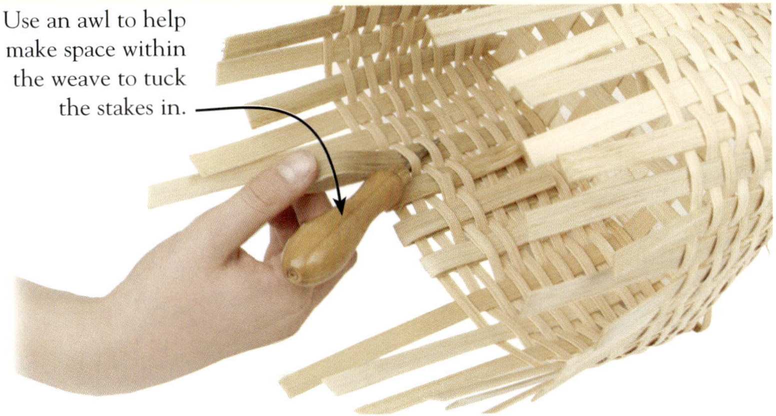

Use an awl to help make space within the weave to tuck the stakes in.

11 Dampen the tops of the stakes. Fold them down inside the basket and slip them under the top couple of rows as shown. Trim the ends to complete the basket.

! Alert

- Awls have sharp points—always store safely.

Drop all your favorite CDs into the box to help keep them in order!

Skill Learned

- Making a square basket
- Start-stop weaving

Super Seagrass Stool

WEAVE A STYLISH seagrass camp stool seat to sit on and have a rest! Seagrass is a rough material and can be tough on your hands, but the seagrass needle makes it easier to work with. The crisscross weaving technique creates a surface that is flexible, comfortable, and extremely strong.

WHAT YOU NEED

TOOLS AND MATERIALS

- Sharp scissors
- Seagrass needle
- Stool frame
- Seagrass

Seagrass needle

1 Put your stool frame together following the instructions that came with it. Tie the end of the seagrass around a bar at the top of the frame.

2 Wrap the seagrass across the top of the stool frame, around the bar on the other side, and underneath both bars back to your starting point.

Knot 2 pieces of seagrass together so that you can continue.

! Alert

- Always point scissors away from you when using them.

Craftsman's Tip

When you knot a new piece of seagrass onto the old piece, make sure you knot it under the bars of the stool frame, so that the knot is hidden on the finished stool.

3 Wrap 4 rows in this way, with each row next to the last. Keep adding rows, in multiples of 4, until you can't fit another 4 onto the stool. Don't pull the seagrass too tight.

4 If you run out of seagrass, tie a new piece onto the old piece, knotting the 2 pieces together as you bring the seagrass under the top bars.

When you reach the end, take the seagrass around the bar at the end and back in between the tunnel of seagrass to the beginning again.

5 When you have wrapped as many rows as will fit, pass the end of the seagrass under the top bar and around the top side bar as shown.

6 Thread the end of the seagrass onto a seagrass needle and pass it under the first 4 rows, over the next 4, and continue going under 4 and over 4 until you get to the end.

7 Make 3 more rows in the same way. On the next row, pass the seagrass over the first 4 rows, then under 4, and over 4 rows to the end. Make 4 rows in this way.

8 Push the rows as close together as possible. Repeat steps 6 and 7, adding rows of seagrass in groups of 4, until you reach the end of the stool.

Fill in the gaps with seagrass.

Craftsman's Tip

You can continue using the seagrass needle to wrap the seagrass around the bar if you find it easier to work with the needle.

9 Fill in the gaps in the weaving on the bars by wrapping the seagrass around the bar.

10 When you have filled in the gaps on 1 side, push the seagrass through the tunnel to the other side to fill in the gaps on that bar. Knot the seagrass around the leg.

See how seagrass creates a neat, as well as strong, woven finish.

Skill Learned

- Seat weaving
- Using a seagrass needle

Coiled Fruit Bowl Basket

This basket is made by wrapping yarn around a seagrass core, and coiling it into a circular shape, creating a super spiral effect! The flexible structure makes it perfect for holding soft objects, such as fruit. Once you have learned the technique, you can experiment with colors and different materials to create a range of coiled baskets.

WHAT YOU NEED

TOOLS AND MATERIALS

- Sharp scissors
- Tapestry needle

- Yarn in 2 colors
- Seagrass

Craftsman's Tip

A tapestry needle is ideal for using when working with yarn, as it has a large eye and a blunt tip.

Knot the ends of the yarn onto the seagrass.

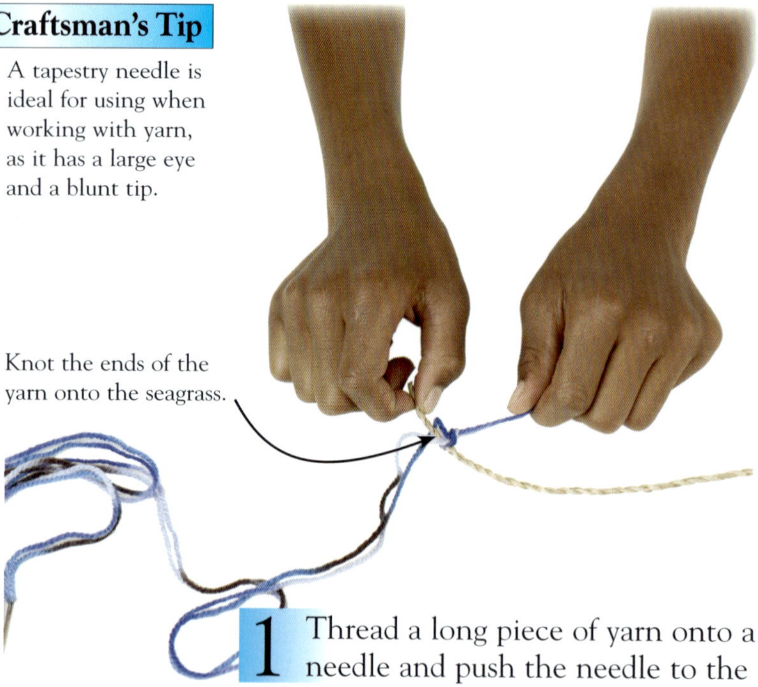

1 Thread a long piece of yarn onto a needle and push the needle to the middle of the yarn. Place the ends of the yarn together and knot them onto the seagrass, about 1" from the end.

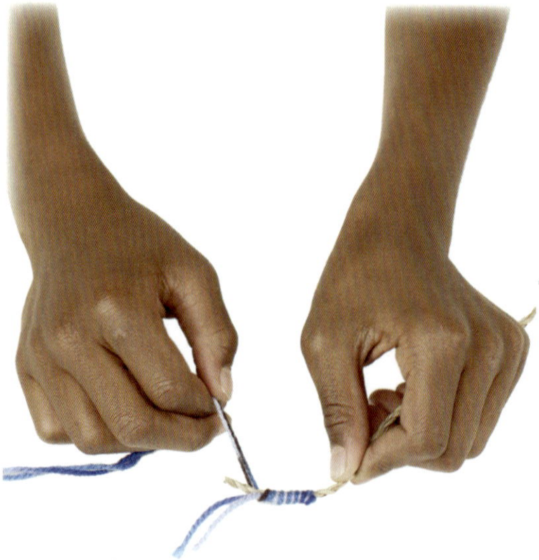

2 Wind the yarn around the seagrass, winding toward the end of the seagrass. Trap the loose ends within the coil and wind around the seagrass 10 times.

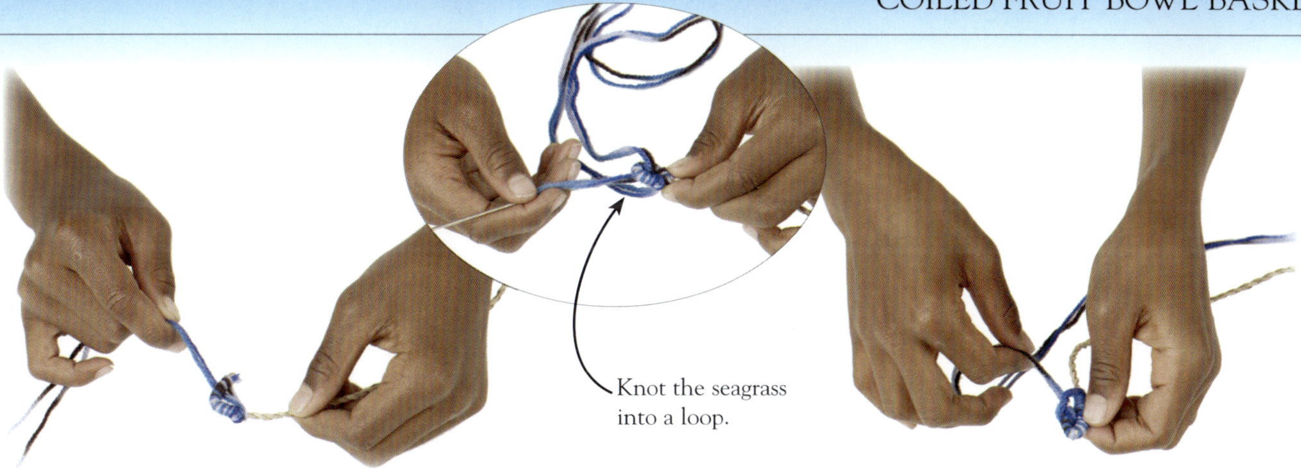

Knot the seagrass into a loop.

3 Bend the wrapped seagrass into a loop and secure it with a knot as shown.

4 Wrap the seagrass with yarn 3 times, then knot the wrapped portion to the looped part with a knot.

! Alert

- Always point scissors away from you when using them.
- Always store needles safely.

Start a new color and hide all the ends under the yarn as you wrap it around the seagrass.

5 Keep wrapping 3 times and knotting the seagrass to the previous row. Create 4 rows in this way.

6 Start a new color by threading the new yarn through the wrapping behind the last knot and wrapping all the ends of the new and old yarn with the new yarn. Wrap and knot 2 rows.

7 Continue wrapping, with 4 rows in 1 color and 2 rows in another until you have 16 rows for the base. Curve the sides upward by holding the new row upright as you knot.

8 Make the bowl as deep as you like. Then, trim the seagrass and place the end on the inside rim. Use several knots with the yarn to cover this end up and secure it to the bowl.

Put your coiled fruit bowl to work and place some fruit inside!

Skill Learned

- Making a coiled basket

Coiled Cone Basket with Lid

USE THE COILING techniques that you learned in the last project and practice your skills to create a funky basket with a lid. See how you can experiment with different shapes as you sew the coils together. Once you have mastered these techniques, there is no limit to the basket creations you can make and the basket fun you can have!

WHAT YOU NEED

TOOLS AND MATERIALS

- Sharp scissors
- Tapestry needle
- Yarn in 2 colors
- Seagrass

! Alert

- Always point scissors away from you when using them.
- Always store needles safely.

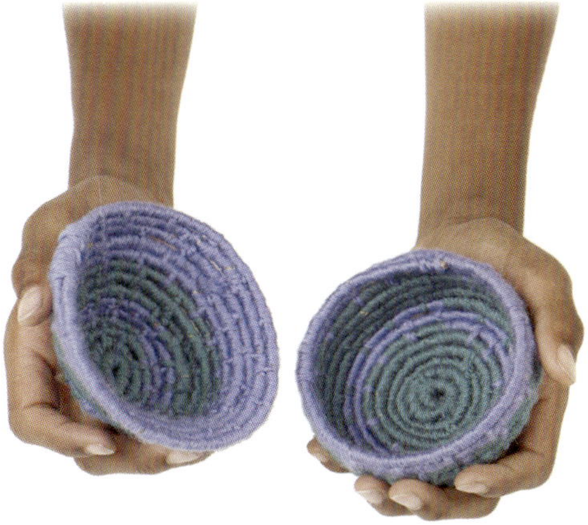

Skill Learned

- Shaping a lid to fit a coiled basket

1 Follow the instructions to make a coiled basket, and make 4 rows in 1 color and 2 rows in another color. Make the rows until the base is 8 rows wide and the sides are 7 rows tall.

2 Make a lid in the same way, but this time coil the basket into a cone shape. Make it big enough for the lid to just overlap the edges of the bottom part of the basket.

Fantastic Fisherman's Hat

LEARN HOW TO make a cool cone-shaped hat that keeps your head cool in the sun, and dry in the rain! In this project, you will twine a flat, circular shape, leaving a segment of the shape unwoven. The weave can then be bent into a cone shape, and straps added, to make an awesome fisherman's hat—see how leaving gaps in the weave can lead to different basket creations.

WHAT YOU NEED

TOOLS AND MATERIALS

- Pencil
- Ruler
- Sharp scissors
- 2 pieces of ribbon/ leather strap

- Masking tape
- *Soak reed before using it*
- 4, 20" pieces of 5 mm round reed (spokes)
- 7, 10" pieces of 5 mm round reed (spokes)
- 1.5 mm round reed (weaver)

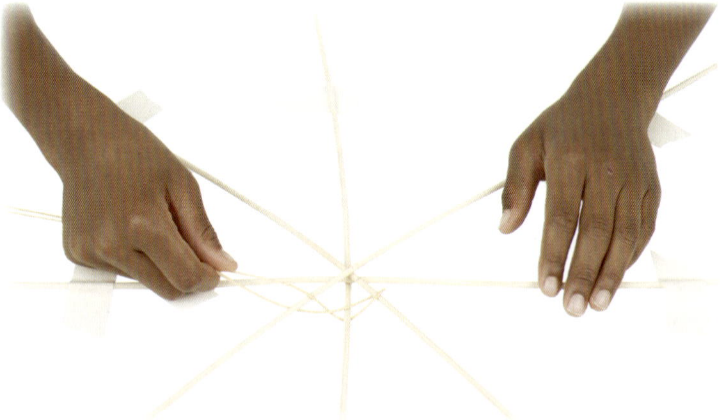

Don't twine all the way around.

1 Mark the centers of the 20" spokes and place them in a star shape. Tape or clip them to the work surface. Start to twine around the stakes with the weaver.

2 Stop twining when you get to the last spoke. Go back and continue twining in the other direction.

3 Twine about 5 rows, back and forth so that 1 segment is left untwined as shown.

Add the extra spokes in between the others.

4 Insert the 7 extra spokes in the gaps between the other spokes, except 1, and twine around all of the spokes individually.

! Alert

- Always point scissors away from you when using them.

You will need to tuck the final spoke in the other way.

5 As before, if you run out of weaver, overlap the old weaver with a new weaver for a couple of spokes and continue. Weave 80 rows and tuck in the ends of the weaver.

6 Dampen all the spokes. Tuck the top of each spoke into the weave, alongside the next spoke along.

Secure the end of the weaver by wrapping it through the weave on 1 side a few times.

7 Dampen the whole hat. Then, bend it around into a cone shape and start to tie the edges together by looping a weaver through the bottom parts of each edge.

8 Tie the 2 sides of the hat together by looping the weaver through the weave all the way to the top. Tie the weaver on the inside of the hat.

Tie your leather strap or ribbon into place.

9 Add a leather strap or ribbon to either side of the hat to hold it on your head. On each side, loop the strap/ribbon around the weave on the inside of the hat and knot it in place.

Skill Learned

- Making a cone shape

Tie the strap under your chin to secure your hat and you're ready to go!

Add some color to your hat with beads. Leave gaps in the weave and place beads on the spokes.

Merry Melon Basket

LEARN HOW TO make a ribbed basket in this project. We'll begin by making a skeleton for the basket and will then weave between the ribs to flesh-out the melon shape. The skeleton also forms part of the handle, which comes in handy for carrying. The melon shape makes the basket ideal for fragile items, like eggs, and precious items, like candy!

WHAT YOU NEED

TOOLS AND MATERIALS

- Pencil
- Ruler
- Sharp scissors
- Binder clips

- *Soak reed before using it*
- 2, 25" pieces of ½" flat reed (for skeleton)
- 4, 12" pieces of ½" flat reed (stakes)
- 2 mm round reed (weaver)
- 3.5 mm round reed (weaver)
- Flat reed (to wrap handle)—we have used $^{3}/_{8}$" flat reed
- Glue

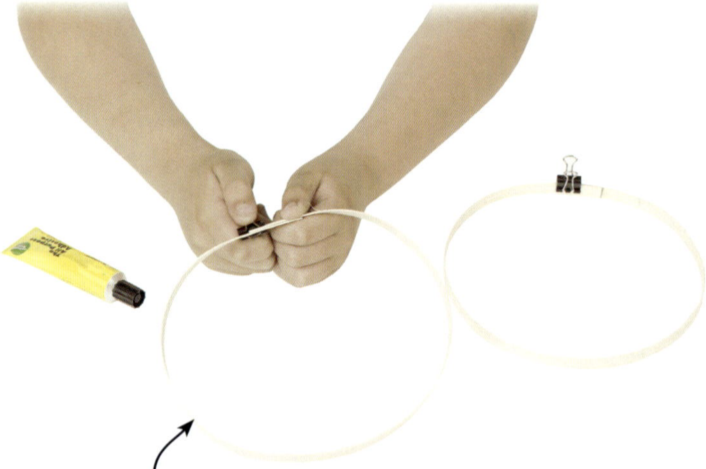

Make 2 hoops to start the skeleton of your melon basket.

1 Mark the 25" pieces of flat reed at 12" and 24". Glue both pieces into hoops so that the ends of each piece meet the 24" marks. Clip the ends together, while they dry.

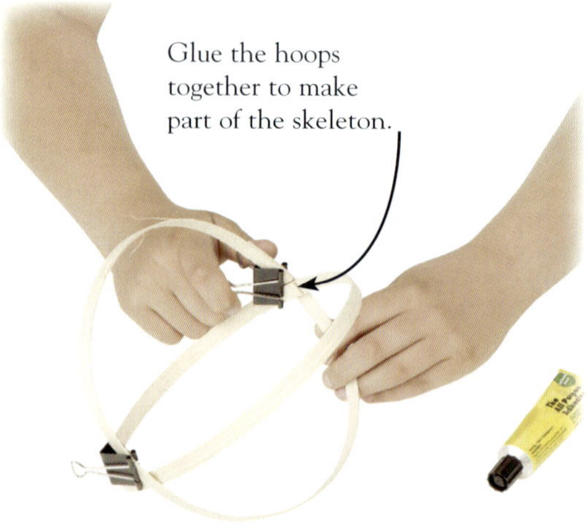

Glue the hoops together to make part of the skeleton.

2 Glue the 2 hoops together so that the pencil marks on each hoop line up. Clip them together and leave them to dry.

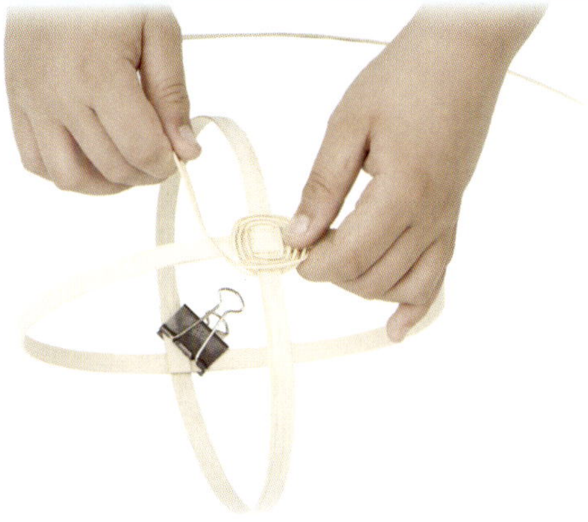

3 At 1 join, twine around the hoops 4 times using the 2 mm round reed.

4 Clip 2, 12” stakes in the gap between the hoops as shown. Twine around them to hold them in place.

! Alert

- Always point scissors away from you when using them.

5 Clip 2 stakes in the next gap and twine around them to hold them in place. Twine around the stakes 4 times as shown. Tuck the weaver into the weave and cut off any excess.

6 Clip the 4 stakes to the other side of the basket and twine around them in the same way as before.

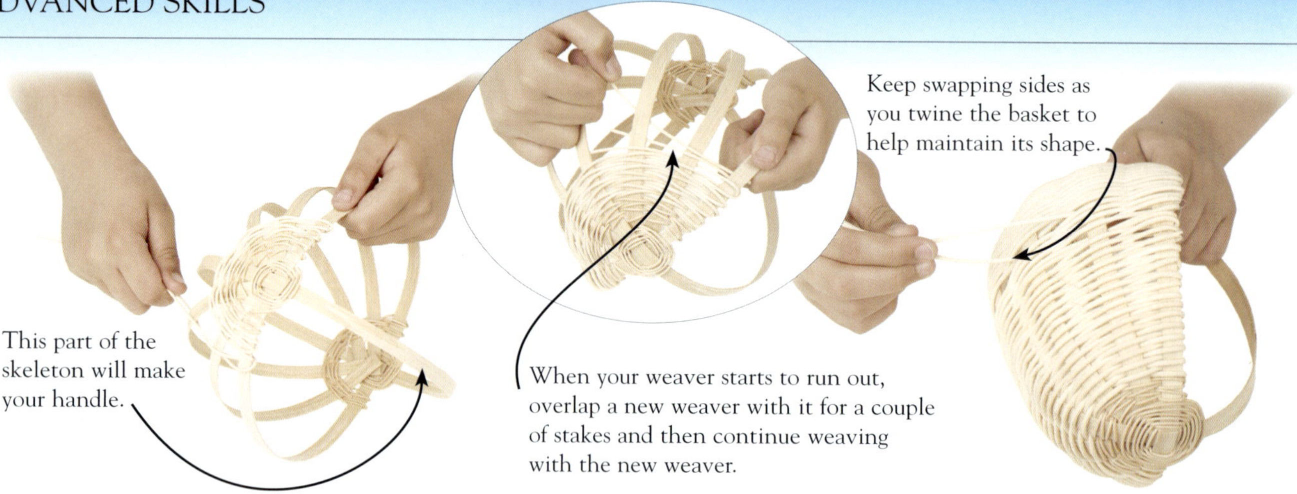

Craftsman's Tip

When twining around the frame, don't pull the reed too tight as it will make the basket lose its shape.

7 Now, twine around the stakes and frame as shown, using the 3.5 mm round reed.

8 Continue, and twine about a quarter of the way across the length of the basket. Then, twine from the other side. Switch sides again and twine each side to the middle of the basket.

Skill Learned

- Making a ribbed basket with a handle
- Twining between ribs

9 Wrap the handle with flat reed and tuck each end into the weave at the ends of the basket to finish.

Wild Willow Tray

START WORKING WITH willow and weave this awesome tray! Willow is a great basketry material that creates a rustic finish for your projects, making them perfect for use in or outdoors. Don't forget that you will need to soak the willow for several hours before you can use it. For this project, you will twist willow sticks into an oval-shaped base, and weave across it to create your tray. Use it as a platter to display your favorite items.

WHAT YOU NEED

TOOLS AND MATERIALS

- Pruning shears
- *Soak willow before using it*
- 4 ft. lengths of willow

Pruning shears

! Alert

- Pruning shears are very sharp—use caution with shears.

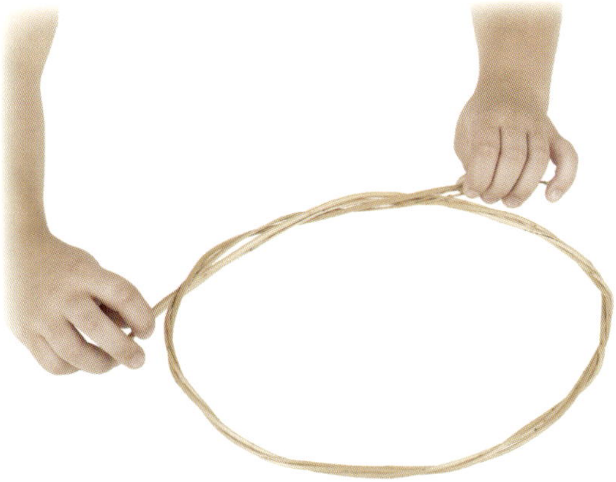

1 Take 3 sticks of willow and twist them together. Then, wind them into an oval loop.

2 Add another stick to the loop, twisting it around the previous sticks. Add 20 sticks in the same way.

Place the sticks in groups of 3 across the oval ring.

3 Select 9 thick sticks. Place them across the top of the oval as shown and trim them so that they just overlap the edge of the oval.

4 Holding the stakes in place, weave another stick over the top rim, under the first 3 sticks, over the next 3, under the next 3, and over the oval rim on the other side.

Keep the stakes straight and grouped together as shown.

5 From the opposite side, weave a stick under the rim, over 3 sticks, under 3, over 3, and under the rim. Straighten the stakes and make sure the weavers are next to each other.

6 Add more weavers, alternating starting over and under the rim until no more can fit on the tray.

7 Trim the weavers and stakes so that they hang just over the rim. Trim any pieces of willow hanging away from the rim.

Willow creates a neat, sturdy finish. Experiment with different shapes and sizes.

Skill Learned

- Working with willow
- Twisting willow into an oval

Wacky Pet Wigwam

TRANSFORM WILLOW STICKS into a wigwam that your pets will love! Learn how to create the frame, twine around the stakes, and leave a gap for the entrance to the wigwam. Once you've mastered the basic skills, try making a larger wigwam for a clubhouse for you and your friends!

WHAT YOU NEED

TOOLS AND MATERIALS

- Pruning shears
- Rubber band

- *Soak willow before using it*
- 6 ft. lengths of willow
- String

1 Select 12 thick willow sticks. Stick them into the ground in a circle, so they stand upright. Bring the tops together and hold them with a rubber band.

Fold the weaver back so that you leave a gap in the weave.

! Alert

- Pruning shears are very sharp—use caution with shears.

Craftsman's Tip

When overlapping a new weaver with an old weaver, try to join thin ends with thin ends and thick ends with thick ends.

2 Fold a thin willow weaver in half and begin to twine around the top. When you run out of weaver, overlap with a new weaver for a couple of stakes and continue.

3 Twine 50 rows. On the next row, twine around 11 stakes, then fold the weaver back and twine around 11 stakes again. Fold the weaver back and continue in this way.

4 Continue for about 30 rows until you are near the bottom. Now, twine all the way around the stakes again for 5 rows.

Secure the bottom together with string.

5 Secure the last few rows with string by looping it around the bottom rows and through the weave. Knot the string at the end.

6 Cut off the stake that is in the middle of the gap. Fold the top part up and tuck it into the weave and remove the bottom part.

7 Cut the bottom stakes so that they are 5" long and trim any twigs sticking out of the wigwam. Push the stakes into the ground to secure it in place.

Neaten any loose ends to finish your perfect pet wigwam.

Skill Learned

- Twining with willow
- Making a large structure
- Weaving with a gap (for the entrance)

Basket Bird Feeder

PUT ALL YOUR basketry skills to the test and make this cool bird feeder! We'll be using similar techniques to those used for the wigwam, but for a much smaller end result. As the bird feeder is made from natural, wood-like materials, it will blend in perfectly in your yard—fill it with food, hang it from a tree, and watch as birds swoop in and out! How many different types of birds can you spot?

WHAT YOU NEED

TOOLS AND MATERIALS

- Pruning shears
- Awl
- Rubber band

- Masking tape
- *Soak willow before using it*
- 4 ft. lengths of willow
- String

Place 8 sticks down on the work surface.

1 Select 8 sticks to use as stakes. Place 4 stakes horizontally and 4 stakes vertically. Tape or clip them to the work surface as shown.

If you run out of weaver, overlap the old weaver by a couple of stakes and continue with the new weaver.

! Alert

- Pruning shears are very sharp—use caution with shears.
- Awls have sharp points—always store safely.

2 Select a thin weaver. Fold it in half and twine it around the stakes in groups of 4. Twine around them 4 times.

3 Divide the stakes into groups of 2 and twine around them twice. Divide the stakes up individually and twine around all the stakes 3 times.

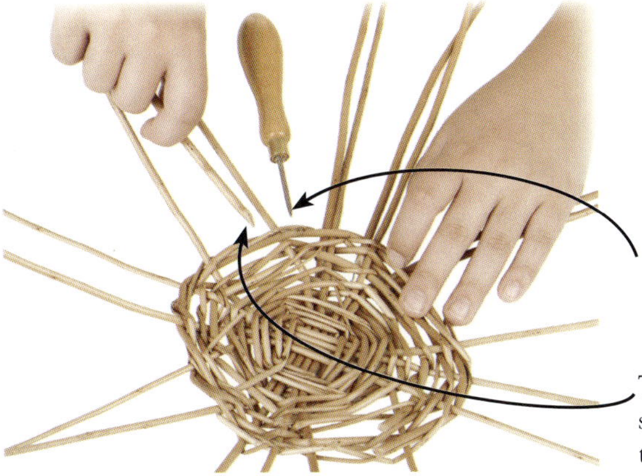

Use an awl to help you tuck the stakes in.

Trim the ends of the stakes to a point to make them easier to insert into the weave.

4 Insert the thick ends of 16 stakes next to each base stake as shown. Cut off the original base stakes and fold the new stakes upward.

5 Hold the stakes upright and tie the tops together with a rubber band. Now, twine around the sides. Twine all the way around 6 times.

Fold the weaver back and continue weaving, so that you leave a gap in the weave.

6

On the next row, twine around 14 stakes, then fold back the weaver and twine the other way for 14 stakes, turn back and continue twining back and forth for 10 rows.

7

On the next row start twining all the way around in a circle again. Twine 10 rows. Trim the 2 stakes at the top and bottom of the gap in the weave.

Tuck the ends of the willow in.

8

At the top, wrap the weaver tightly around the outside of the stakes up to the point where they all meet. Tuck in the ends of the weaver.

9

Tie string through the weave at the back of the feeder so that you can hang it up.

Hook your bird feeder up on a tree branch in your yard, add some food and watch the birds!

Skill Learned

- Creating a closed basket with a hole (for the birds to get in to)

Glossary

base
The bottom of a basket.

cane
A material used for weaving, which is made from a plant called rattan.

continuous weaving
Weaving that goes continuously around the sides of a basket and doesn't stop between rows. An odd number of stakes are needed for continuous weaving.

"cross" base
A circular base in which the stakes have first been laid out in a cross shape, and are then gradually separated into a circular shape during weaving.

lasher
A thin piece of reed, or other basketry material, which is used to hold the rim of a basket in place.

lashing
The process of securing a rim onto a basket by looping the lasher around the rim and through the basket weave.

over-under (or plain) weaving
A method of weaving in which the weaver is passed over a stake, under the next and so on.

rattan
A vine-like plant that is found in many rain forest areas. Rattan is often made into cane and reed.

reed
The inner core of the rattan plant that has been cut and processed into long coils of flat, round, flat-oval, half round, or oval material and is used in baskets and for furniture.

ribs
The pieces of a basket that extend from one side to the other and form the skeleton of the basket.

rim
A flat piece of reed that is attached around the top of a basket.

seagrass
A long, narrow plant that grows underwater. Strands of seagrass can be twisted and used for weaving.

spoke
A piece of material that is used in a round or oval basketry base. Spokes are often laid in a circle (as in the spokes of a wheel) and woven around to make the base of a basket.

stake
A piece of material that is "upset" to become an upright part of the basket around which the weavers are woven.

"star" base
A circular base in which the spokes have been laid out in a star shape.

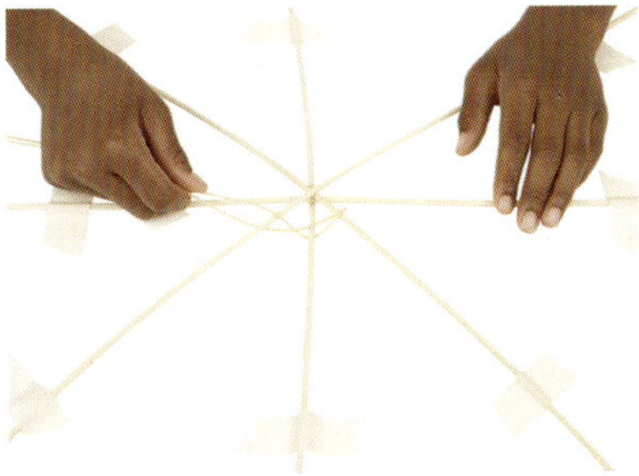

start-stop weaving
Weaving in which a new weaver is used for each row. An even number of stakes are needed for start-stop weaving.

twill weaving
Similar to over-under weaving, but the weaver is taken over, then under, two or more stakes at a time.

twining
A method of weaving using two weavers that alternate between the front and back of each stake.

upset
To bend stakes up and back on themselves, to create fixed stakes for the sides of the basket.

weaver
The material that is woven around the stakes, spokes, or ribs to make the basket.

weaving
Passing flexible strips (weavers) in and out between fixed stakes.

Index

Picture Credits
(b=bottom, c=center, l=left, r=right, t=top)
6bl, Marek Pawluczuk / Shutterstock Images LLC; 9bl, Alexey Averiyanov / Shutterstock Images LLC; 9tr, (pine needles) Artem Rebrov / Shutterstock Images LLC; 9br, (raffia) Robert Adrian Hillman / Shutterstock Images LLC.